# Teaching With State Quarters

BY KAREN BAICKER

SCHOLASTIC
Teaching
Resources

NEW YORK • TORONTO • LONDON • AUCKLAND • SYDNEY
MEXICO CITY • NEW DELHI • HONG KONG • BUENOS AIRES

*In memory of the tic-tac-toe playing chicken,*
*who knew the value of a quarter.*

*Many thanks to my wonderful editor, Kama Einhorn.*

Cover design by **Norma Ortiz**
Interior design by **Holly Grundon**
Cover art by **Estefania Hecht-Toltl, Lucy Schmitz, Jacob Schmitz, Hallie Borstel**

ISBN: 0-439-51372-3

2 3 4 5 6 7 8 9 10    40    10 09 08 07 06 05 04 03

# Contents

# Using State Quarters
## in the Classroom

Kids are natural-born collectors. Whether it's rocks, shells, stuffed animals, baseball caps, or trading cards, most kids have something they're "into"! Although that habit can produce messy backpacks and bedrooms, the desire to collect serves an important developmental process. Kids learn to sort, organize, and assign value as they begin their collections. They also learn to share an interest with others.

Schools sometimes prohibit trading cards and other collectibles, for obvious and legitimate reasons. But collecting can help build social and emotional skills. Just as philatelists (stamp collectors) and numismatics (coin collectors) flock to conventions, kids will huddle at the playground to discuss and trade the latest hot item. In doing so, they are participating in a common culture.

Most of your students are probably familiar with the United States Treasury's State Quarters program. Many may "collect" them in one form or another—in a jar on their dresser, or in a folder with press-in coin holes. As a teacher, there are many ways you can tap into this natural interest. At the younger grades, you can teach about coins, value, and basic addition and subtraction. For the older grades, the coins offer opportunities to teach history, geography, math, economics, citizenship, and more.

By encouraging students' interest in the State Quarters, you are introducing a hobby that crosses cultures and generations. Students might be able to share their interest with a grandparent who collects coins. After all, coin collecting is the oldest hobby in the history of the world!

You can also build classroom community through a coin collection. Students can join together in keeping their eyes open for the latest state coin. You might start a Quarter Drive for a local charity. You can design your own school coins, commemorating important people and events in your school's history. And, if your state's quarter has not been released, you might present a real proposal to the U.S. Mint (see page 30).

This book is divided into four different content areas (Math and Economics, Geography, History, and Language Arts) and addresses other topics, such as science and citizenship, throughout. Many of the activities correlate with the National Standards for these topics, including NCTM and NCSS. Suggestions for literature, Web sites, software, and other resources can also be found throughout the book. You may also wish to copy the Family Letter (page 8) to alert families to the opportunities that the State Quarter program can offer at home.

Happy collecting!

# All About the
# State Quarters Program

In 1999, the United States Mint launched its State Quarters program with the release of the Delaware State Quarter. In an unprecedented program, the U.S. quarter's design will change five times a year, for ten years. Every ten weeks, through 2008, the U.S. Mint will release a new State Quarter, until every state is represented with its own design.

## In what order will the quarters be released?

The coins are being released in the order in which the states were ratified. Delaware was chosen as the first state coin because it was the first state to join the Union by ratifying the United States Constitution in 1787.

Each coin will be minted and released only during its ten-week period. It will then go out of production, and the U.S. Mint will release the next coin. During this time, the "Eagle" quarter (minted until 1999) will not be produced. After all fifty states are released, the Washington quarter will go back into production. On pages 6–7 you'll find a chart showing the release schedule. You can distribute the My State Quarters checklist (pages 24–25) for students to research and record this information.

The state quarters all feature George Washington on the front, just as the Eagle quarters do. The back of each state coin will have a new design, chosen to represent the history of that state.

## How are the designs for the quarters chosen?

The government has issued general guidelines for the design of the quarters. Within those limits, states get to choose their own designs, in a process that varies from state to state. Frequently, officials from the state government contact artists to request submissions. Often the process is open to all citizens of the state. Note that the design is selected at least two years before the release date. You can check your state government's Web site (usually **www.yourstate.gov**, substituting your state's name in the middle) to find out if your state is soliciting submissions.

You can find proposed designs for upcoming quarters as well as the designs of already-produced quarters at **http://www.quarterdesigns.com/index.html**. You can also place your own vote through that site. Encourage students to create their own designs, using the reproducible on page 30.

## ONLINE RESOURCES

The U.S. Mint's Web site, **www.usmint.gov**, includes detailed information about the program and its history. You can also find lesson plans on this site.

Another excellent resource for teachers is the U.S. Department of Treasury's Web site, **www.treas.gov**.

# State Quarters
## Fact Sheet

| State/ Release Date | Joined the Union | Quarter | State/ Release Date | Joined the Union | Quarter |
|---|---|---|---|---|---|
| **Delaware** 1999 | December 7, 1787 | | **North Carolina** 2001 | November 21, 1789 | |
| **Pennsylvania** 1999 | December 12, 1787 | | **Rhode Island** 2001 | May 29, 1790 | |
| **New Jersey** 1999 | December 18, 1787 | | **Vermont** 2001 | March 4, 1791 | |
| **Georgia** 1999 | January 2, 1788 | | **Kentucky** 2001 | June 1, 1792 | |
| **Connecticut** 1999 | January 9, 1788 | | **Tennessee** 2002 | June 1, 1796 | |
| **Massachusetts** 2000 | February 6, 1788 | | **Ohio** 2002 | February 19, 1803 | |
| **Maryland** 2000 | April 28, 1788 | | **Louisiana** 2002 | April 30, 1812 | |
| **South Carolina** 2000 | May 23, 1788 | | **Indiana** 2002 | December 11, 1816 | |
| **New Hampshire** 2000 | June 21, 1788 | | **Mississippi** 2002 | December 10, 1817 | |
| **Virginia** 2000 | June 25, 1788 | | **Illinois** 2003 | December 3, 1818 | |
| **New York** 2001 | July 26, 1788 | | **Alabama** 2003 | December 14, 1819 | |

| State/<br>Release Date | Joined<br>the Union | Quarter | State/<br>Release Date | Joined<br>the Union | Quarter |
|---|---|---|---|---|---|
| **Maine**<br>2003 | March 15, 1820 | | **Nebraska**<br>2006 | March 1, 1867 | |
| **Missouri**<br>2003 | August 10, 1821 | | **Colorado**<br>2006 | August 1, 1876 | |
| **Arkansas**<br>2003 | June 15, 1836 | | **North Dakota**<br>2006 | November 2, 1889 | |
| **Michigan**<br>2004 | January 26, 1837 | | **South Dakota**<br>2006 | November 2, 1889 | |
| **Florida**<br>2004 | March 3, 1845 | | **Montana**<br>2007 | November 8, 1889 | |
| **Texas**<br>2004 | December 29, 1845 | | **Washington**<br>2007 | November 11, 1889 | |
| **Iowa**<br>2004 | December 28, 1846 | | **Idaho**<br>2007 | July 3, 1890 | |
| **Wisconsin**<br>2004 | May 29, 1848 | | **Wyoming**<br>2007 | July 10, 1890 | |
| **California**<br>2005 | September 9, 1850 | | **Utah**<br>2007 | January 4, 1896 | |
| **Minnesota**<br>2005 | May 11, 1858 | | **Oklahoma**<br>2008 | November 16, 1907 | |
| **Oregon**<br>2005 | February 14, 1859 | | **New Mexico**<br>2008 | January 6, 1912 | |
| **Kansas**<br>2005 | January 29, 1861 | | **Arizona**<br>2008 | February 14, 1912 | |
| **West Virginia**<br>2005 | June 20, 1863 | | **Alaska**<br>2008 | January 3, 1959 | |
| **Nevada**<br>2006 | October 31, 1864 | | **Hawaii**<br>2008 | August 21, 1959 | |

# Dear Families,

Your child will be exploring the State Quarter program at school this year to learn about history, geography, language arts, and math. As you may know, the United States Mint has been issuing new quarters to represent each state. Each state will have its own design on the back, chosen to reflect its culture, geography, or history. The program was launched in 1999 and will continue through 2008, releasing five new quarters each year.

The State Quarters are exciting to kids! It's fun to look for the newest designs and figure out what they represent. It's fun to try to collect every quarter, and to place them on a map of the United States.

By using Scholastic's *Teaching With State Quarters* program, we are hoping to take advantage of your child's natural enthusiasm for the new quarters. We will flip coins to study probability, design our own state quarters, work with fractions, make timelines, and learn about our nation's history.

You can help by encouraging their interest in State Quarters at home. Start a quarter collection. Talk about the designs on the back of each coin and what they represent. Look at the dates that they entered the Union (shown on the back of each coin) and discuss what was happening in our country at that time. Get out a map or globe and locate the different places.

Coin collecting is also a hobby your child may share with other relatives and friends. Encourage your child to talk about his or her interest with others. If someone in the family has a collection of coins (or stamps), we would welcome a classroom visitor!

Please let me know if you have any questions about the State Quarters program.

Sincerely,

# Teaching
## Math & Economics

### Coins, Numbers, and Value

Help students make the distinction between number and value.

Value is an important math concept that has broader applications than just coins and money. Number refers to numerals on a page (1, 2, 3, and so on). Value refers to the amount that those numbers represent. This can be a tricky distinction for students to grasp, and coins can be a great way to convey the concept. For younger students, start by reviewing their basic identification skills. Make sure that they can recognize pennies, nickels, dimes, and quarters.

Show them four quarters, ideally from different states. (You can use the reproducible State Quarters on page 23, instead of real quarters.)

Ask students how many coins there are. (4) Tell them that they have just told you the *number* of coins. Now ask them how much the coins are worth. (*one dollar*) Let them know that they have just given you the *value* of the coins. You can extend the activity with different configurations of coins, asking these same questions with one quarter, two quarters, and so on.

Add other coins to the mix and have students repeat the activity in pairs or small groups, with one student playing "teacher." You can also create a chart showing number and value for different coins, and ask students to add up the grand total.

Page 23

## Literature Link

**Benny's Pennies** by Pat Brisson (Doubleday, 1995). Benny sets off with five new pennies to spend and eventually finds something for his mother, brother, sister, dog, and cat.

## State 1/4s

Demonstrate the concept of "quarters" in a variety of ways.

Start by taking a square sheet of paper and folding it in half. Hold it up and show your students "halves." Then fold it again in the opposite direction, hold it up, and show "quarters." You can let them know that this fraction can also be called "fourths." Write the fraction 1/4 on the chalkboard. (You can also fold the square sheet along the diagonals, to make four triangles.)

Many simple origami projects begin with these basic quarter folds. Show your students how to make "fortune tellers" and jumping frogs—two easy origami projects that feature quarter folds. You can find complete instructions at **http://www.enchantedlearning.com/crafts/origami**.

Ask students to think of other ways to represent quarters as well: wedges in a pie, 15-minute blocks on a clock, seasons of the year. Then, discuss the fact that four quarters equal one dollar. Thus, each is 1/4 or a quarter. Depending on the level of your students, show them the following equations as different ways of viewing a dollar:

$$25 + 25 + 25 + 25 = 100$$
$$25 \times 4 = 100$$
$$100 \div 4 = 25$$
$$25 = 1/4 \ 100$$
$$100 - 25 - 25 - 25 - 25 = 0$$

## Krypto

Play a variation of the card game Krypto.

Tell students that they have a target number, 25. Then give them four other numbers that they can use to try to reach that target number. They can use any operation: addition, subtraction, multiplication, or division. But, they must use each number once, and only once. For example, write the numbers 10, 20, 5, and 1 on the board. To reach the target number, 25, make the equation: $10 + 20 - 5 \times 1 = 25$.

Then, play a version of this using coins. Put out pennies, nickels, and dimes and challenge students to come up with equations that total a quarter.

Sheet of paper folded in fourths

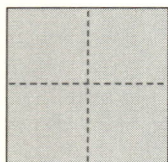

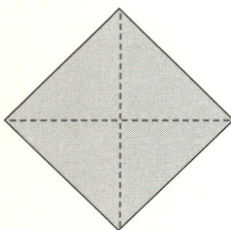

### Cents & Nonsense!

A dollar bill is good for measuring in a pinch. They are just slightly longer than 6 inches (6.14 inches, to be precise)! Want to go Metric? That's 15.5 centimeters.

## Roll of the Dice

To teach kids about coin value, play a simple game with dice.

Play this game with a small group of students. Use real coins or the reproducible coins on page 23. Let each student try to "earn" a quarter. Students take turns rolling a number cube. Give them pennies equal to the number they roll. When they have five pennies, they can turn them in for a nickel, and so on, until they have a quarter. This will help students understand that more coins do not necessarily equal more money!

### Literature Link

**The Great Tooth Fairy Rip-Off** by Dori Hillestad (Fairview Press, 1999). A boy tries to negotiate with the Tooth Fairy for the value of his tooth, but the Tooth Fairy strikes a hard bargain. In the process, the boy learns the values of work, money, and savings.

### Cents & Nonsense!

A stack of dollar bills one mile high would contain 14.5 million dollars. If you had 10 billion one dollar bills, you could spend one dollar every second for 317 years before running out of money. See if students can write an equation that calculates this fact!

## Heads I Win

Flipping coins is a great way to teach probability.

Take out a coin and flip it. Ask students to raise their hands if they think it's heads. Write down the number of students who guess heads, and then the number who guess tails. (You can use the correct coin terminology, and ask them to guess *obverse* and *reverse*. See the glossary on page 31.) Tell them that each of them has a 50% chance of being correct.

Reveal the answer to the flip. Let them know that if you flip the coin again, the chances are still 50% for heads, 50% for tails. If you flipped the coin eight times and got eight heads, you'd still have a 50% chance of getting heads the next time.

However, if you ask students, "What are the odds that I'll flip two heads in a row?" the answer is not 50%. It's 25%. The reasoning for this is a little complicated, but students third grade and older may be able to understand it. Show them the four options for two flips using a diagram on the chalkboard.

**Page 31**

Have students work in small groups and record the results of their flips in columns showing heads and tails. Collect the sheets and analyze the results as a group. Note that the levels should even out with a broader sample; that is, you will be more likely to approach a 50/50 split if you flip more quarters.

## Release Math

*The United States Mint releases a new quarter every ten weeks.*

Pose "timely" math problems that reinforce fractions, percentages, multiplication, and division. Ask:

- How many quarters will be released in a year? (5)
- How many weeks remainder? (2)
- How many weeks will it take to release all the states? (500)
- How many years will it take to release all the coins? (10)
- What percentage of coins has been released so far?
  *(Answers will vary according to when you ask. See pages 6–7.)*

See pages 6–7.

## CENTS & NONSENSE!

Depending on the design for each state quarter, the odds of heads or tails might *not* actually be 50/50. The design might "tip the scales" toward one side. Experimenters have found that the Euro coin is not evenly weighted for each country. Encourage students to conduct experiments with different state quarters.

## CENTS & NONSENSE!

Not all metal is magnetic. U.S. coins are made from non-magnetic metals. Some coins from other countries are magnetic; the Brazilian 50-centavo piece is made from steel.

## Science Connection
## Metal Mix

Discuss the different alloys (combinations of metals) from which coins are made. Metals were originally used because they had attained value within many societies. (Metal was scarce, and thus valuable.) This chart shows the combinations of metals currently used in U.S. coins. You can show students a periodic table of the elements and let them write each coin's composition in scientific terms. To see a table of the elements, go to **www.webelements.com**.

| Penny | 97.5% zinc, 2.5% copper |
|---|---|
| Nickel | 75% copper, 25% nickel |
| Dime | 91.67% copper, 8.33% nickel |
| Quarter | 91.67% copper, 8.33% nickel |
| Half-dollar | 91.67% copper, 8.33% nickel |
| Sacagawea Golden Dollar | 88.5% copper, 6% zinc, 3.5% manganese, 2% nickel |

## Compare and Contrast

Ask students to look for differences between the traditional "Eagle" quarter (the production of which has stopped until the end of the State Quarter Program) and the new state quarters. The words "United States of America," "Quarter Dollar," "Liberty," and *E Pluribus Unum* have been moved to the obverse (heads) side on the State Quarters. The obverse still shows George Washington. See page 31.

## Literature Link

For younger students, reinforce the values of coins with **The Coin Counting Book** by Rozanne Lanczak Williams (Charlesbridge Publishing, 2001).

## Art Connection
### Making Dough

Coins are made by heating metals and pressing them into thin sheets. They are then cut, cookie-cutter style, by machines into blank coins (or *planchets*). Ridges are then added to the blanks with another machine. Then designs are pounded into the coins. To simulate the process, follow this simple dough recipe:

| | |
|---|---|
| 2 cups flour<br>1 cup salt<br>food coloring of choice<br>1/2 cup water | Mix together, then let students roll and "mint" their own coins! |

### Coin Rubbings

Let students make coin rubbings. It's a good way for tactile learners to get a feel for the coins! Distribute pieces of blank white paper. (Ordinary typing paper or newsprint work fine; construction paper is too thick for effective rubbings.) Have students place the paper over a coin and rub until the pattern emerges. (Let them use the sides of crayons with the wrappers removed, or the edge of a pencil.) Then have them repeat with other coins and make a coin collage. They can also write and draw a "number story" with coin rubbings: two dimes + one nickel = one quarter.

### Cents & Nonsense!

The ridges on the edge of coins were originally devised to protect them from cheats. When coins were made with silver and gold, people could secretly shave bits off of the coins and sell the precious metals. The ridges made it obvious if someone tried to shave the coin.

# Teaching
## Geography

### Locating States

Copy and distribute the outline map of the United States (pages 26–27). Have students identify your state and locate it on the map. Then ask them to color in the map key.

Discuss what region your state is in, what states border it, and other geographic facts about your state's location. Use a world map or globe to make sure that younger students understand the relationship between town, state, country, continent, and world.

Distribute the reproducible sheet of State Quarters (page 23). Ask students to cut out the quarters and glue them onto the correct states.

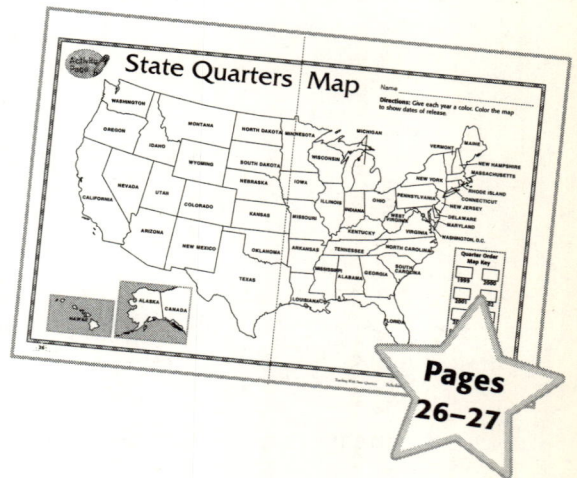

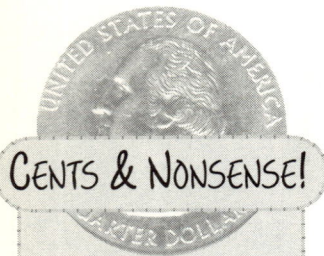

Pages 26–27

### Using a Compass Rose

Copy and distribute the State Quarters map (pages 26–27).

Ask students to identify the relative locations of different states. For example, what is the state directly south of New Hampshire? Then try the same activity incorporating coin trivia. For example: Suppose Caesar Rodney (see sidebar, left) wanted to ride to see the Charter Oak. Which direction would he travel?

Encourage students to make up direction questions for each other. Invite them to draw their own compass rose and label the direction points.

**CENTS & NONSENSE!**

The Delaware State Quarter shows a man on horseback. Many people identify this rider as Paul Revere. In fact, the patriot shown is Caesar Rodney. At the age of 70, Rodney galloped many dangerous miles, through a storm, high waters, and mud, to cast the deciding vote in the Continental Congress.

## State Geography

Students examine geographical patterns.

The quarters are being released in the order in which the states were ratified. Ask students to consider what geographic factors might have influenced the order of states' entry into the union. (Locations near oceans and rivers; Southern versus Northern states) Point out that most of the early states were among the original thirteen colonies. The colonies were located along the Atlantic Ocean—accessible to the colonists who came by boat from Europe. Have students fill in and examine the columns of release dates (pages 24–25) to look for other patterns related to geography. See pages 6–7 for release date information.

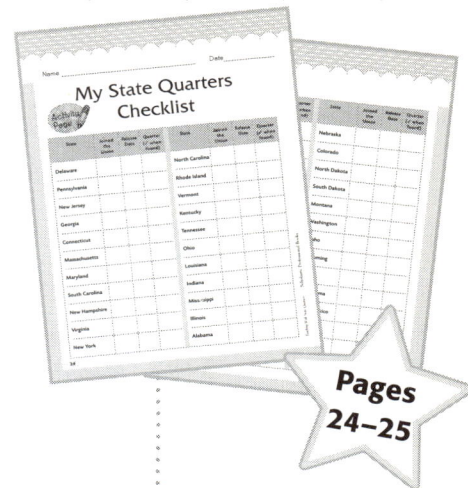

Pages 24–25

# History/Geography Connection
## Two Sides of the Same Coin

Some states chose historical events to represent on their quarters. Others have chosen geographic elements, including important landforms, crops, plants, and animals. Some combine elements. For example, New Jersey's coin shows Washington crossing the Delaware. It depicts an historical event that was influenced by geography! Ask students to look through the quarters issued so far and categorize them according to what they are commemorating. How many coins so far represent geographic aspects of the state?

As they review the designs, they will notice that it is often hard to make a clear distinction between geography and history. Explore the ways that these two disciplines are interconnected.

## Facts About the 50 States

Students create State Quarters Collector Cards.

Distribute large blank index cards or rectangles of oak tag. Ask each student to choose four states and create cards for them. They can use an almanac to gather information for their cards, including State Quarter design, year of statehood, state symbols, and other trivia.

Then students can collect and trade their cards. You can also create a State Trivia game using the cards. Divide the class into two teams. Collect the cards from each team (keeping them separate). Quiz the different teams using the other teams' cards.

## State Symbols

Many states have incorporated their state symbols in their coin designs.

Ask students whether they know what your state's symbols are—and then let them know some of the ones they aren't familiar with.

Discuss the fact that state symbols are usually designated through the state government. Often, a bill is presented before the state legislature, debated, and voted on, before it officially becomes a state symbol.

Most states have an official tree, bird, and plant. But some states go further and even have state muffins! Ask students to write a bill proposing a new symbol for your state. Make sure their proposal includes an explanation for why this item is symbolic of your state.

## Your State Geography Here

Students suggest geographical facts that could be depicted on your state quarter (whether your state's quarter has been designed or not).

Ask students to write a paragraph explaining why they think the feature should be depicted.

Then ask them to show a design for that idea, using the Design-a-Quarter reproducible (page 30). Point out the official guidelines for state quarter designs, summarized on that activity page. Have students vote on the ideas and designs. You can incorporate this geography activity with history as well (see page 18).

### CENTS & NONSENSE!

Every dollar bill has a serial number in the upper right and lower left part of the bill. No two notes of the same series and denomination have the same serial number.

## Art Connection
### Making a Relief Map

Make a salt-clay landform map of the United States, and embed quarters in the clay in the appropriate states. Leave indentations to add future coins.

First, draw an outline of the U.S. map on heavy cardboard or wood.

For the dough, mix 2 parts salt and 1 part non-rising wheat flour. Slowly add 1 part water, while stirring. Add food coloring if you want—make some green, brown, and blue.

Make the map soon after mixing the dough. Cover the entire map area with one layer and then build layers of elevation up from there, using a topographic map for reference. Let layers dry as you go. Press the quarters in and let dry for several days. Paint if desired.

# Teaching
# History

## State Quarters Timeline

Students reinforce their knowledge of the dates on which states joined the union.

Distribute copies of pages 6–7. Use a long strip of tagboard. Start by looking at each coin, in the order in which they've been released. If the design depicts an historical event, illustrate that event on your timeline. Also add the date that the state joined the union.

Have students participate in gluing each coin to the timeline, and discuss the historical events that were occurring around that time period. Or, you can tape pictures of each state's quarter next to the event described on the timeline.

Have students study the list of dates that each state joined the union (pages 6–7). Explore different patterns. For example, the first states on the list are all clustered around December 1787 and January 1788. Ask students if they know why there were so many states formed around that time. (That was the time of the signing of the Constitution.) What important treaty led to Louisiana's statehood in 1812? (the Louisiana Purchase) What historical event happened in 1821, that created a new state? (the Missouri Compromise)

### CENTS & NONSENSE!

The Federal Reserve offers a free service. If you have cash that has been burned, torn, or otherwise destroyed, they will help you verify and replace that money. Once, a farmer sent his cow's stomach to them, stuffed with money!

## Math Connection
## Graph It!

You can incorporate state quarters into many different graphing activities. Ask students to make a simple bar graph to record how many states entered the union during each ten-year period. You can also create a simple two-bar graph showing the number of states released and yet to be released.

## CENTS & NONSENSE!

### THINGS THAT HAVE BEEN USED FOR MONEY

**Chocolate bars** (in Europe after World War II)

**Cowrie shells**

**Feathers**

**Ivory**

**Salt** (hence the word salary, from the Latin word for salt, *salarius*)

**Tobacco** (the official currency of the Virginia colony)

**Wampum** (from the Algonquin language: *wab* meaning "white" and *umpe* meaning "string")

**Stones** (the Japanese Yap stones, also known as *fei* stones, were giant coins up to 12 feet in diameter and weighing as much as 500 pounds)

## Your State History Here

Students suggest historical events that could be depicted on a State Quarter for your state.

**A**sk students to write a paragraph explaining why they think a certain historical event should be commemorated. Then ask them to show a design for that idea (copy page 30 for each student).

Page 30

## History of Money

Share the following information with students. They might also create a timeline showing the history of money.

◆ The first known government mint was created by King Croesus, of Lydia (western Turkey), between 560 and 546 B.C. Lydians used a gold and silver alloy, known as electrum. The alloy was cast into disks and then placed on an anvil. A design was then hammered onto each coin, using an engraving of a figure.

◆ In the middle ages, there was a kind of coin chaos. Different kings, princes, and dukes all had their own mints, even within the same country. In the 1400s, France had over 50 different mints at the same time. Over time, countries found it was better to standardize their coinage. That way, they could use their money for trade with other countries.

◆ The thirteen British Colonies made their own money, the New England shillings, in 1652. They were about the same size as a quarter. One side had the letters NE. The other showed the coin's value in Roman numerals. The United States Constitution standardized and nationalized the coinage, so that states were no longer allowed to mint their own coins. Today, mints in Philadelphia and Denver produce almost all of our nation's coins.

◆ The Euro is a relatively new coin. The Euro provides one standard currency that can be used throughout the nations in Europe without the need to convert.

## History of the Quarter

Share the following information with students.

◆ The Philadelphia Mint produced the first quarter in 1796. These first quarters were solid silver. But in 1873, Congress determined that the coins were not heavy enough. They added extra silver to make it heavier. Coins stayed the same until 1965. That year, the Mint Act of 1965 allowed for the use of a copper-nickel alloy instead of silver.

◆ For the first 115 years, the quarter featured the word "Liberty" and an image of "Lady Liberty." This image was changed many times to keep up with changes in other coins, and with changes in the times. The eagle on the reverse also was modified. (At one point people thought it looked too much like a pigeon!)

◆ In 1932, to commemorate the bicentennial of George Washington's birth, Washington's silhouette took over the obverse. In 1976, to commemorate the nation's bicentennial, an image of the Declaration of Independence was issued. And on the reverse, a colonial drummer replaced the eagle.

◆ All these changes are very few relative to the scope of the current commemorative State Quarters program!

Have students make a State Quarters timeline showing the different versions of the quarter that have been issued. They can find these quarters at **www.usmint.gov**. Encourage them to find out what events prompted each redesign of the quarter.

### CENTS & NONSENSE!

The Susan B. Anthony Dollar was a silver dollar coin that quickly fell out of favor. The coin was too similar in size and color to the quarter, so it was too often confused for a quarter. The Sacagawea Dollar was introduced in 2000, in honor of the Native American woman who helped Lewis and Clark on their historical expedition.

## Multicultural Connection
### Money All Over

Let students explore the different kinds of money that are used across of the world, as well as the different kinds that have been used over time (see Cents & Nonsense! sidebar, right). Discuss the creation of the Euro, a currency that ties the countries of Europe together with a common unit of currency.

# Teaching
## Language Arts

### Write a State Poem

Students create state poems based on word-associations with your state. Create a word web as a graphic organizer to help them get going!

Create a large web on the chalkboard and fill it in as a class, or help students create individual webs. Have them fill in the web with key words and phrases and then write a poem about your state. Check your state government's Web site to see if your state has an official state poem.

### Coin Poems

The American Numismatic Society (ANS) sponsors a National Coin Week every year in April.

April is also National Poetry Month, so the American Numismatic Society solicits Haikus in honor of the two celebrations. Haikus are a Japanese form of poetry. They feature three lines with 5, 7, and 5 syllables per line. Have students write their own Haikus. Here is one from the ANS Web site, **www.money.org.**

### Coins

Gold, silver, copper . . .
what stories they hold for those
who study them well.

---

## CENTS & NONSENSE!

Funny Money: Parker Brothers has printed more money for its Monopoly games than the Federal Reserve has issued in real money for America. If you stacked up all the Monopoly sets they have made, the pile would be over 1,100 miles tall.

## The Tails Tell the Tale!

Each state quarter tells a story.

**D**ivide students into small groups. Distribute real quarters or the reproducible coins on page 23, giving each group a different coin. Ask them to create stories based on the images shown. Their stories should suggest why the image was chosen for the state quarter—but the reason can be based on imagination. Distribute the Coin Glossary (page 31) as well, and encourage students to incorporate new terms.

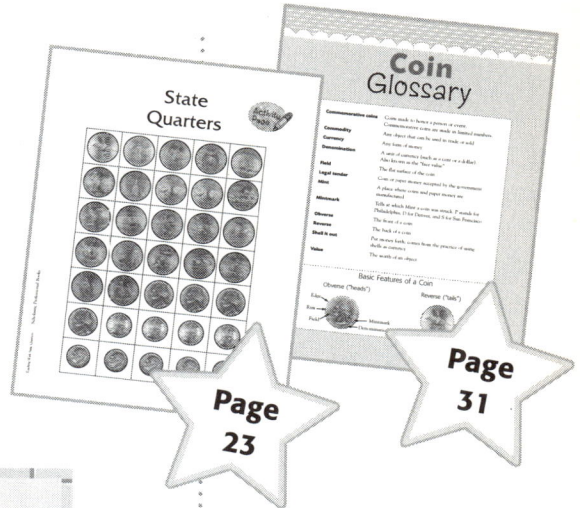

**Page 23**

**Page 31**

## Literature Link

Most states have folk tales about their origins from early Native American groups. Read **Stories from Native North America** by Linda Theresa Raczek (Raintree, 1999).

## Brain Teasers and Crosswords

**D**istribute the Trivia & Brain Teasers reproducible (page 29) and the State Quarters Crossword Puzzle (page 28) and have students work individually or in small groups to solve them. Then have students create their own State Quarters word problems and present them to each other.

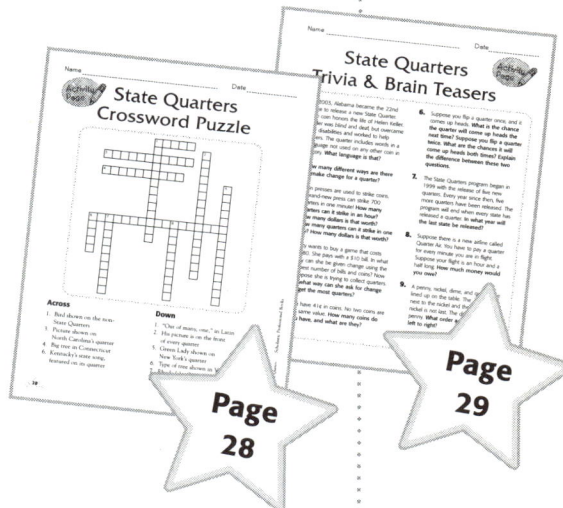

**Page 28**

**Page 29**

### Crossword Answers

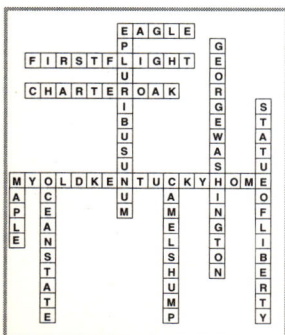

### Trivia Answers

1. Helen Keller's name is spelled out in Braille, a language of raised dots that blind people read with their fingers.
2. 11
3. 42,000 in one hour, worth $10,500
1,008,000 in 24 hours, worth $252,000
4. for the fewest number of coins and bills: 1 five, 1 one, and 2 dimes; for the most quarters: 24 quarters and two dimes
5. one penny, one nickel, one dime, and one quarter
6. 50%; 25%
7. 2008
8. $562.50
9. nickel, quarter, dime, penny

## Coin a Phrase

There are many expressions in our culture
that come from money terms.

- Broke
- Strapped for cash
- Pennies from heaven
- Put your money where your mouth is
- Don't take any wooden nickels

- Other side of the coin
- Dough
- Money talks
- Stop on a dime
- Dime store

Have students write a short story using as many money terms as possible. Distribute the glossary on page 31. Encourage them to use those phrases and vocabulary words as well.

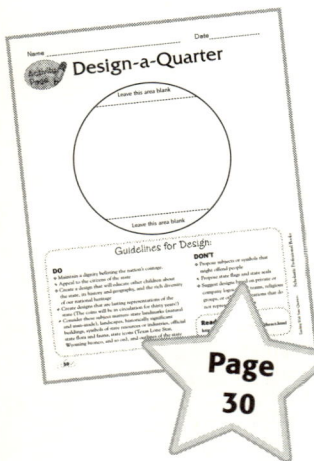

**Page 30**

## Art Connection
### Design a Coin

Use the Design-a-Quarter reproducible (page 30) to have students create their own designs for quarters or other coins. Design a class coin. What images come to mind when students think about the class? What symbols might represent the group?

## Citizenship Connection
### Write a Bill

Review with students the process by which a State Quarter design gets chosen. Go to the United States Mint Web site (**www.usmint.gov**). Point out that other state symbols are often chosen through the legal steps by which a bill becomes a law: someone proposes the symbol, the state legislature votes on it, and the governor signs the bill. Ask students to propose a state symbol in the form of a bill. You can vote on a school mascot and follow the same steps used by your state.

# State Quarters

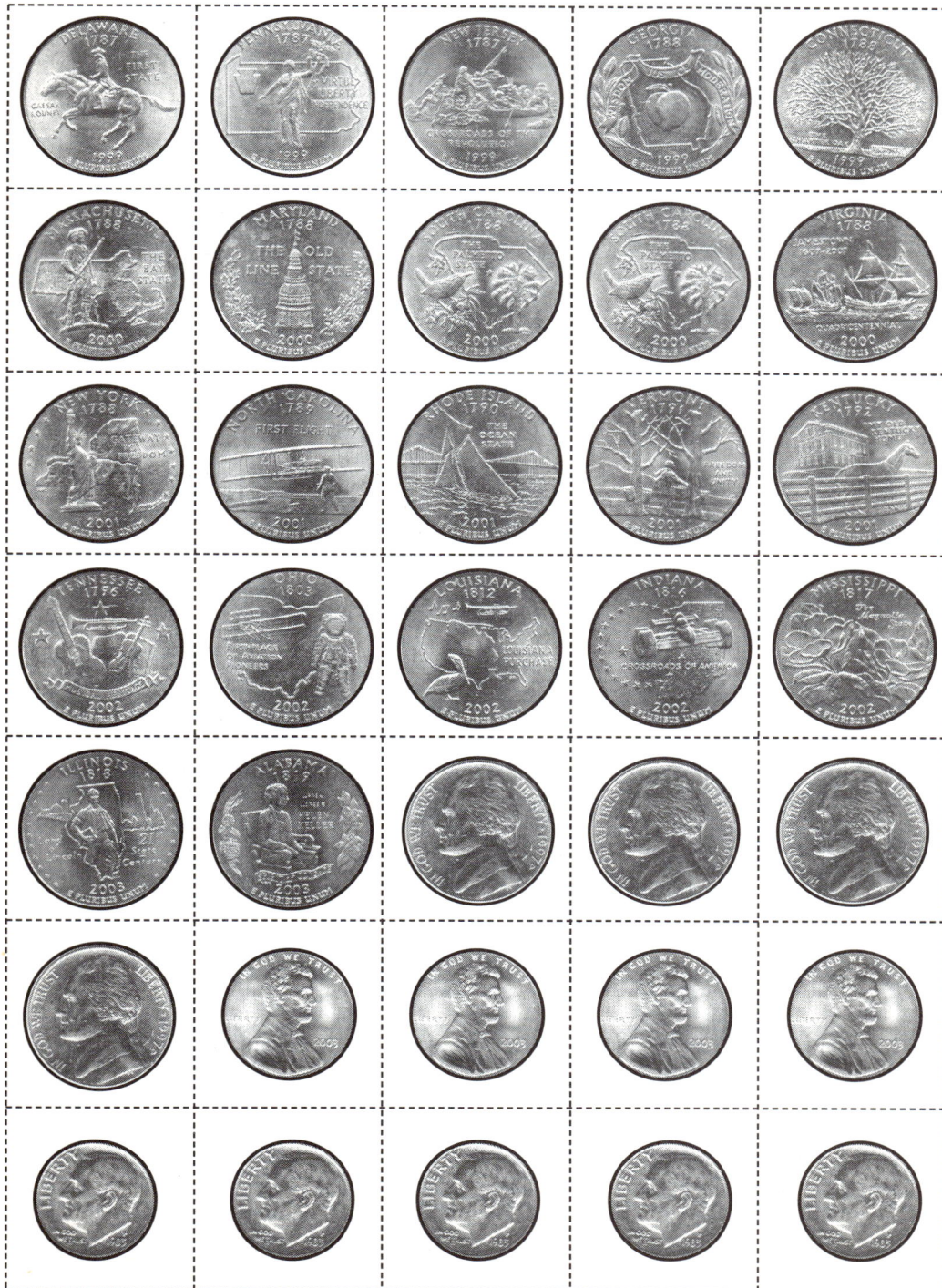

Name _____  Date _____

# My State Quarters Checklist

Activity Page

| State | Joined the Union | Release Date | Quarter (✓ when found) | State | Joined the Union | Release Date | Quarter (✓ when found) |
|---|---|---|---|---|---|---|---|
| Delaware | | | | North Carolina | | | |
| Pennsylvania | | | | Rhode Island | | | |
| New Jersey | | | | Vermont | | | |
| Georgia | | | | Kentucky | | | |
| Connecticut | | | | Tennessee | | | |
| Massachusetts | | | | Ohio | | | |
| Maryland | | | | Louisiana | | | |
| South Carolina | | | | Indiana | | | |
| New Hampshire | | | | Mississippi | | | |
| Virginia | | | | Illinois | | | |
| New York | | | | Alabama | | | |

Teaching With State Quarters      Scholastic Professional Books

| State | Joined the Union | Release Date | Quarter (✓ when found) | State | Joined the Union | Release Date | Quarter (✓ when found) |
|---|---|---|---|---|---|---|---|
| Maine | | | | Nebraska | | | |
| Missouri | | | | Colorado | | | |
| Arkansas | | | | North Dakota | | | |
| Michigan | | | | South Dakota | | | |
| Florida | | | | Montana | | | |
| Texas | | | | Washington | | | |
| Iowa | | | | Idaho | | | |
| Wisconsin | | | | Wyoming | | | |
| California | | | | Utah | | | |
| Minnesota | | | | Oklahoma | | | |
| Oregon | | | | New Mexico | | | |
| Kansas | | | | Arizona | | | |
| West Virginia | | | | Alaska | | | |
| Nevada | | | | Hawaii | | | |

# State Quarters

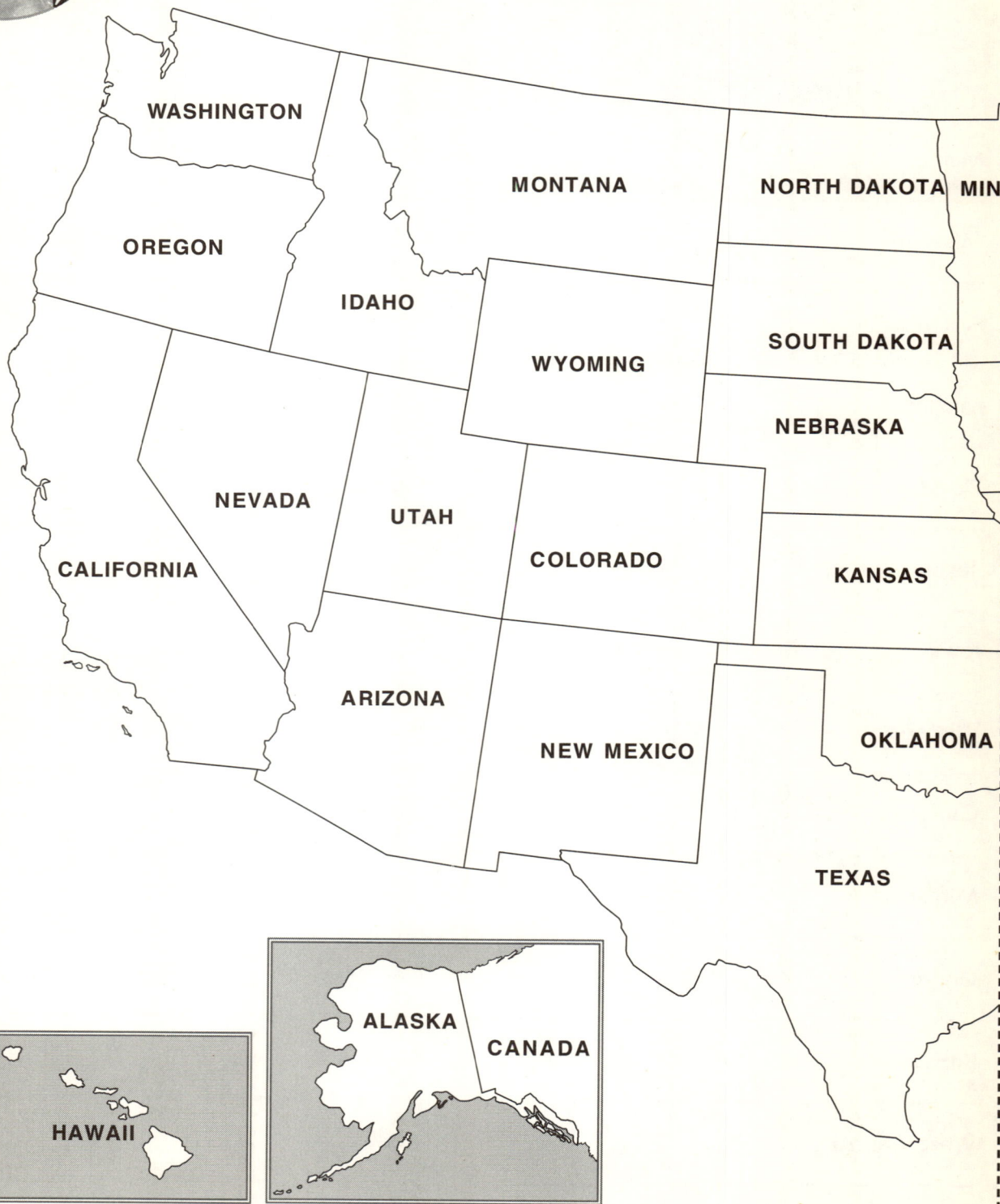

WASHINGTON

OREGON

MONTANA

IDAHO

NORTH DAKOTA    MIN

WYOMING

SOUTH DAKOTA

NEBRASKA

NEVADA

UTAH

COLORADO

KANSAS

CALIFORNIA

ARIZONA

NEW MEXICO

OKLAHOMA

TEXAS

HAWAII

ALASKA

CANADA

cut here

# Map

Name _____

**Directions:** Give each year a color. Color the map to show dates of release.

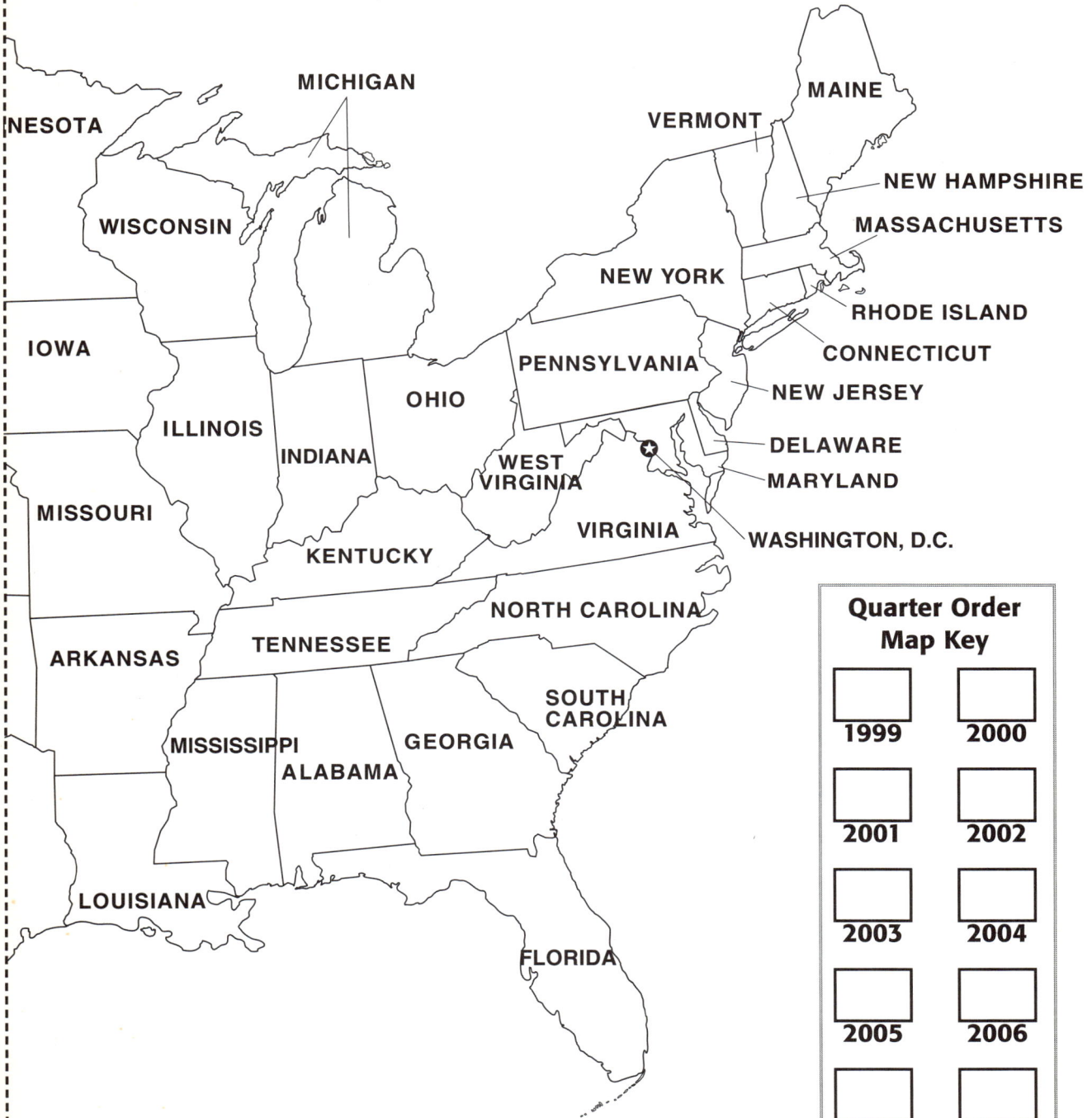

MICHIGAN

MAINE

VERMONT

NESOTA

NEW HAMPSHIRE

WISCONSIN

MASSACHUSETTS

NEW YORK

RHODE ISLAND

IOWA

PENNSYLVANIA

CONNECTICUT

NEW JERSEY

OHIO

ILLINOIS

DELAWARE

INDIANA

WEST VIRGINIA

MARYLAND

MISSOURI

VIRGINIA

KENTUCKY

WASHINGTON, D.C.

NORTH CAROLINA

ARKANSAS

TENNESSEE

SOUTH CAROLINA

MISSISSIPPI

GEORGIA

ALABAMA

LOUISIANA

FLORIDA

## Quarter Order Map Key

| | |
|---|---|
| 1999 | 2000 |
| 2001 | 2002 |
| 2003 | 2004 |
| 2005 | 2006 |
| 2007 | 2008 |

cut here

# State Quarters Crossword Puzzle

**Activity Page**

## Across

1. Bird shown on the non-State Quarters
3. Picture shown on North Carolina's quarter
4. Big tree in Connecticut
6. Kentucky's state song, featured on its quarter

## Down

1. "Out of many, one," in Latin
2. His picture is on the front of every quarter
5. Green Lady shown on New York's quarter
6. Type of tree shown in Vermont
7. Rhode Island's nickname
8. Mountain shown for the "Green Mountain State"

Scholastic Professional Books

Teaching With State Quarters

# State Quarters Trivia & Brain Teasers

**1.** In 2003, Alabama became the 22nd state to release a new State Quarter. The coin honors the life of Helen Keller. Keller was blind and deaf, but overcame her disabilities and worked to help others. The quarter includes words in a language not used on any other coin in history. **What language is that?**

**2.** **How many different ways are there to make change for a quarter?**

**3.** Coin presses are used to strike coins. A brand-new press can strike 700 quarters in one minute! **How many quarters can it strike in an hour? How many dollars is that worth? How many quarters can it strike in one day? How many dollars is that worth?**

**4.** Lucy wants to buy a game that costs $3.80. She pays with a $10 bill. In what way can she be given change using the fewest number of bills and coins? Now suppose she is trying to collect quarters. **In what way can she ask for change to get the most quarters?**

**5.** You have 41¢ in coins. No two coins are the same value. **How many coins do you have, and what are they?**

**6.** Suppose you flip a quarter once, and it comes up heads. **What is the chance the quarter will come up heads the next time? Suppose you flip a quarter twice. What are the chances it will come up heads both times? Explain the difference between these two questions.**

**7.** The State Quarters program began in 1999 with the release of five new quarters. Every year since then, five more quarters have been released. The program will end when every state has released a quarter. **In what year will the last state be released?**

**8.** Suppose there is a new airline called Quarter Air. You have to pay a quarter for every minute you are in flight. Suppose your flight is an hour and a half long. **How much money would you owe?**

**9.** A penny, nickel, dime, and quarter are lined up on the table. The quarter is next to the nickel and the dime. The nickel is not last. The dime is next to the penny. **What order are they in, from left to right?**

Name _____     Date _____

# Design-a-Quarter

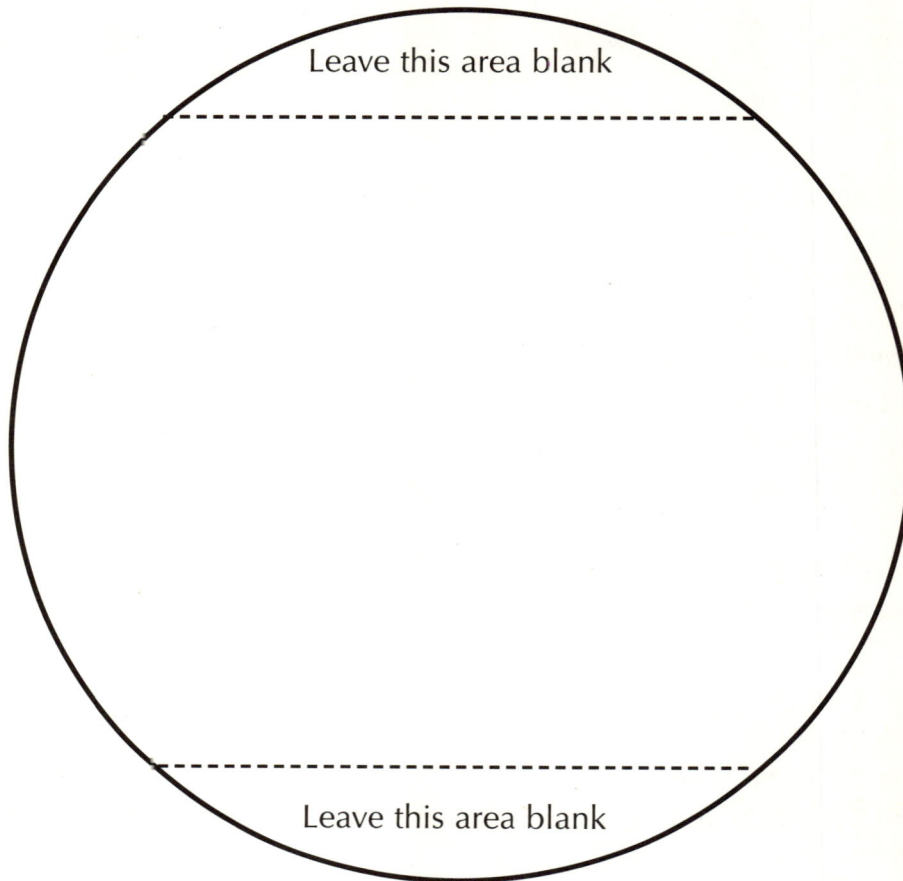

*Activity Page*

Leave this area blank

- - - - - - - - - - - - - - - - - - - - - -

Leave this area blank

## Guidelines for Design:

### DO

◆ Maintain a dignity befitting the nation's coinage
◆ Appeal to the citizens of the state
◆ Create a design that will educate other children about the state, its history and geography, and the rich diversity of our national heritage
◆ Create designs that are lasting representations of the state (The coins will be in circulation for thirty years!)
◆ Consider these subject matters: state landmarks (natural and man-made), landscapes, historically significant buildings, symbols of state resources or industries, official state flora and fauna, state icons (Texas Lone Star, Wyoming bronco, and so on), and outlines of the state

### DON'T

◆ Propose subjects or symbols that might offend people
◆ Propose state flags and state seals
◆ Suggest designs based on private or company logos, sports teams, religious groups, or other organizations that do not represent all citizens

### Read the Act
http://www.quarterdesigns.com/theact.html

Scholastic Professional Books

*Teaching With State Quarters*

# Coin Glossary

| | |
|---|---|
| **Commemorative coins** | Coins made in limited numbers to honor a person or event. |
| **Commodity** | Any object that can be used in trade or sold |
| **Currency** | Any form of money |
| **Denomination** | A unit of currency (such as a cent or a dollar), also known as the "face value" |
| **Field** | The flat surface of the coin |
| **Legal tender** | Coin or paper money accepted by the government |
| **Mint** | A place where coins and paper money are manufactured |
| **Mintmark** | Tells at which Mint a coin was struck. P stands for Philadelphia, D for Denver, and S for San Francisco |
| **Obverse** | The front of a coin |
| **Reverse** | The back of a coin |
| **Value** | The worth of an object |

## Basic Features of a Coin

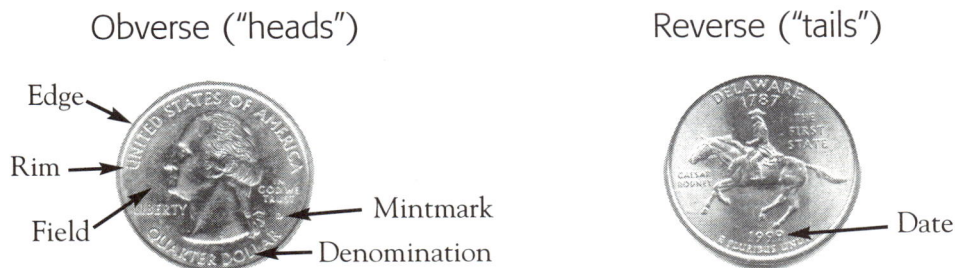

### Obverse ("heads")

Edge
Rim
Field
Mintmark
Denomination

### Reverse ("tails")

Date

# Resources

## Books

*The Coin Counting Book* by Rozanne Lanczak Williams (Charlesbridge, 2001) (ages 4–8)

*The Go-Around Dollar* by Barbara Johnston Adams (Four Winds Press, 1992)

*The Great Tooth Fairy Rip-Off* by Dori Hillestad (Fairview Press, 1999)

*The Magic of a Million Activity Book* by David M. Schwartz and David J. White (Scholastic, 1998)

*A Quarter from the Tooth Fairy* by Caren Holtzman (Scholastic, 1995) (ages 4–8)

*Benny's Pennies* by Pat Brisson (Doubleday, 1995) (ages 4–8)

*If You Made a Million* by David M. Schwartz (Mulberry, 1994) (ages 4–8)

*A Dollar for Penny* by Julie Glass (Random House, 2000) (ages 4–8)

## Software

Coin Critters (Nordic Software) (ages 5–12)

Dollarville (Waypoint Software) (ages 5–9)

## Web sites

www.wdfi.org/ymm/kids/history/ includes a chronological history of money.

www.usmint.gov is the official site of the U.S. Mint.

www.funbrain.com/cashreg is an online cash register game.

http://superkidz.com/money.html has great teaching resources.

www.money.org and www.amnumsoc.org both feature detailed information for coin collectors.